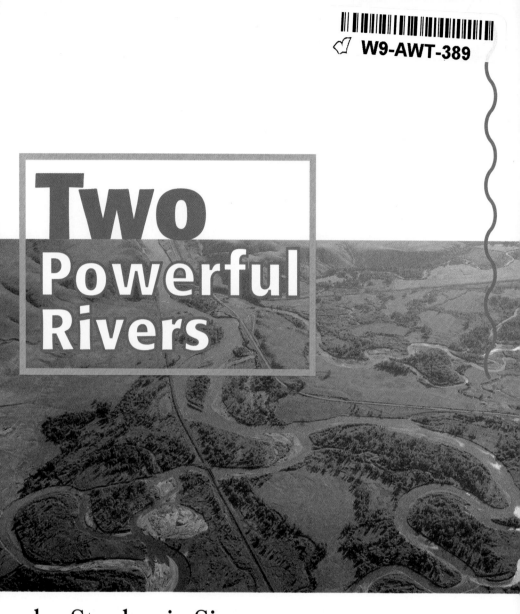

Two Powerful Rivers

by Stephanie Sigue

Scott Foresman
is an imprint of

Glenview, Illinois • Boston, Massachusetts • Chandler, Arizona
Upper Saddle River, New Jersey

ISBN 13: 978-0-328-51629-2
ISBN 10:   0-328-51629-5

The Mighty Mississippi

The Mississippi River is one of the most famous rivers in the world. It is the widest river in the United States and the second longest. Mark Twain gave a vivid description of the river in his book *Life on the Mississippi*. Many other writers, poets, and songwriters have been inspired to write about it.

The Mississippi River is divided into three parts: the Headwaters, which is where the river begins, the Upper Mississippi River, and the Lower Mississippi River. This river begins as a small stream from Lake Itasca in northern Minnesota. It flows from north to south for over two thousand miles and passes through many states before emptying into of the Gulf of Mexico.

Two great United States rivers

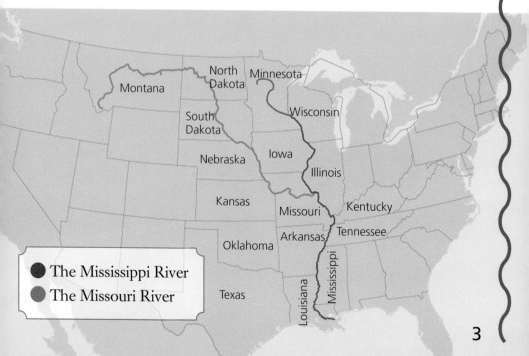

The Mississippi River
The Missouri River

3

As the Mississippi meanders along, it is joined by the waters of several other rivers. The Minnesota, St. Croix, Wisconsin, Rock, Illinois, Missouri, Ohio, Arkansas, Yazoo, and Red Rivers all meet the Mississippi somewhere along the way. More than 250 **tributaries** from the east and west flow into the Mississippi. It is no wonder that so many Native American tribes–the Illinois, the Kickapoo, and the Ojibway, among others–that lived in the upper Mississippi Valley called it "Big River" and the "Father of Waters."

History of the River

The Mississippi was formed about 100,000 years ago. At that time glaciers covered the Northern Hemisphere. As the glaciers began to melt, they carved out channels. Meltwater filled the channels to form the Mississippi River.

Hernando de Soto, a European explorer, crossed the river in 1541 near what is now Memphis, Tennessee. Later, French explorers traveled the river and claimed the Mississippi Valley for France. Finally, the United States bought the western Mississippi basin from France in the Louisiana Purchase of 1803.

Hernando de Soto

The river was an important transportation and trade **route.** After the development of steamboats in the early 1800s, the river became even more important. Cities along the river–St. Louis, Memphis, and New Orleans–became the best places to buy supplies before heading west.

The Louisiana Purchase

In the 1800s, railroads and bridges were built to make it easier to cross the river. However, the river continued to be a major trade route. River transportation increased in the early twentieth century. Using tugboats and **barges,** large quantities of cargo and freight began to be transported along the great river.

The locks, or gates, in this section of the Mississippi River raise and lower the water level so that ships can pass through.

More than 60 percent of the United States' grain exports are carried down the Mississippi River each year. Aluminum, petroleum, coal, and steel products are transported on the river. Even food, such as corn, soybeans, and wheat, moves along the Mississippi.

The port of New Orleans is the busiest port in the United States. You can sit on the wharf and scan the city's docks as ships from all over the world are loaded and unloaded. The Mississippi is also popular with tourists. Steamboat and riverboat cruises provide wonderful views of the river and its surrounding beauty.

Tourists ride a riverboat along the scenic Mississippi River.

Floods and Flood Control

Flooding along the Mississippi can be a problem. When melting snow or heavy rains add lots of water to the river, the river overflows its banks. If the surrounding land is unable to absorb the water, flooding occurs. Since many acres of wetlands along the river have been drained and turned into farmland, more water has been forced into the river. Paved roads, parking lots, and even the roofs on buildings prevent rainwater from soaking into the ground. This increases run-off into the river and the chance of flooding. Severe flooding often results in damage to nearby homes and communities.

Several methods are used to control floods. One way is to plant trees, grass, and other plants to absorb the water. Another way to control flooding is to build levees. Levees raise the banks of the river so that it can hold more water. Floodways are areas of land that provide outlets for draining water when the river reaches flood level. They help to decrease flooding elsewhere.

Levees help flooding control along the Mississippi.

Flood water from the
Mississippi River engulfs the
city of Keithsburgh, Illinois.

Plant and Animal Life

Forests and wetlands border much of the Mississippi River. These natural areas provide important habitats for plants, fish, and wildlife.

The clear waters of the upper Mississippi are home to freshwater fish such as bass, sunfish, and trout. In the muddy waters of the lower Mississippi, carp, catfish, and buffalo fish make their home. The coastal wetlands of Louisiana provide areas where oysters, crabs, and shrimp are raised.

Wildlife is found along most of the Mississippi. More than four hundred species of animals live along this stretch of water. Mink, muskrats, opossums, otters, skunks, and rodents called nutrias live in the swamps and marshlands along the Mississippi Delta. Forty percent of the nation's migrating birds flock to the area during the winter. These include ducks, geese, and other migratory birds. Pelicans, herons, and egrets live in the area year-round.

A nutria in the wild

Dangers to the River

The Mississippi River has faced two problems. One is the amount of sediment that flows into the Mississippi from the Missouri River. The construction of a series of reservoirs along the Missouri, however, now traps sediment and stops it from flowing into the river.

Pollution is another problem. Poor water quality threatens the habitats of many plant and animal species. Wildlife was threatened when fertilizers and chemicals were washed into the river from farms and factories. Now the government has made regulations that control the use and disposal of harmful chemicals that damage the environment.

Great blue heron (left); Mississippi alligator hiding among the lily pads (below)

The Muddy Missouri

The Missouri River is not as famous as the Mississippi River, but it's longer. It flows 2,315 miles through seven states, starting from the Jefferson River at Red Rock Creek in southwestern Montana.

The Platte River in Nebraska is the largest of the Missouri River's tributaries. Other major rivers that flow into the Missouri are the Big Sioux, Cheyenne, James, Kansas, Milk, Osage, and Yellowstone.

Native Americans and early explorers called the river "Big Muddy" because of the amount of mud in the water. The name, Missouri, probably comes from the name of the Indian village *Ou-Missouri* or *Oue Messourit,* which was located near the mouth of the river.

Gateway Arch in St. Louis, Missouri, on the Mississippi riverfront

Aerial view of the headwaters
of the Missouri River

Missouri River History

The Wind River Shoshone and Atsina Native American nations lived near the headwaters of the Missouri in western Montana. The river was a hunting ground, a canoe route, and a source of water.

French explorers Louis Joliet and Father Jacques Marquette were most likely the first to explore the eastern Missouri in 1673. Later, in 1738, another group of French explorers traveled the upper parts of the river. They reported seeing herds of buffalo and Native American villages in the area that would later become North Dakota.

Lewis and Clark

In 1803 President Thomas Jefferson chose Meriwether Lewis and William Clark to lead an **expedition** that would take them from Missouri to the Pacific Ocean. Jefferson wanted them to form peaceful relations with the Native American tribes along the way and to establish trade with them. The expedition also was to gather and record information. Jefferson wanted to know about the geography of the terrain, the types of plants and animals they found, and the mineral resources.

Lewis and Clark's expedition began in May of 1804 and ended in September of 1806. During that time they met Sacagawea, the Shoshone wife of a Canadian fur trapper. She helped guide them up the Missouri River and across the Rocky Mountains.

Lewis and Clark exploring in the Bitterroot Mountains in Montana (above)

An antique wooden compass with leather pouch used on the expedition (right)

The River and Its Uses

The Missouri River has an upper, middle, and lower part. The upper Missouri, near Montana, is a clear mountain stream. The middle part of the river begins when the river leaves the mountains and crosses the Great Plains. This part of the river is slower and muddier. The lower part of the river is the slowest and muddiest of all. It begins in South Dakota and flows until the Missouri and Mississippi meet near St. Louis.

The river is muddy because it picks up sand as it moves through the mountains. The river runs over a thick bed of **silt** and carries the silt to the Mississippi. Much of the mud and silt is trapped by reservoirs on the Missouri River, but some of it empties into the Mississippi. Before meeting the Missouri, the Mississippi is actually clear.

The Missouri River has always been a trading route. In earlier times fur traders moved furs from the West to the East on the river. Today most of the river traffic above Sioux City, Iowa, is recreational. The activity on the lower part of the river is commercial. Between Sioux City and St. Louis, tugboats push barges loaded with farm and industrial products.

Big Bend Dam at Fort Thompson, South Dakota

No More Floods

Wherever there is a large amount of free-flowing water, there is a danger of flooding. However, this danger has been addressed along the Missouri River. Six huge dams were built on the river to form a chain of **reservoirs.** These reservoirs are positioned from north to south along the river. They are at Fort Peck, Garrison, Oahe, Big Bend, Fort Randall, and Gavins Point. There are also sixty smaller dams and reservoirs along the Missouri's tributaries that keep the Missouri from overflowing.

Besides **diminishing** the chances of flooding, the dams provide electrical power to the farms, homes, and factories along the river's banks. The reservoirs provide recreation spots too. Boating, fishing, waterskiing, swimming, and other water sports are all popular.

Missouri River Wildlife

Where the Missouri runs through the mountains, bear, elk, deer, moose, and other large animals are plentiful. In the middle and lower parts of the river valley, smaller animals are more common. These include beavers, foxes, muskrats, and weasels.

Rainbow trout and mountain whitefish live in the parts of the river that are clear. Bass, catfish, carp, and perch live in the muddier waters.

Environmental Dangers

Today **conservationists** and the federal government disagree about how much water should flow into the river. Conservationists think that some fish and wildlife are in danger if the water flow is controlled by the dams. They want the natural flow of the river restored.

Conservationists say that the high level of water necessary to support barge traffic is harmful to animals. It floods the nesting habitats of two species of endangered river birds and reduces the survival rate of an endangered fish. A court will have to decide the outcome. For now the dam system continues to be used.

A white-tailed deer fawn in a Missouri tall grass prairie (top) and a mink by the water in Montana (bottom) are samples of wildlife found along the Missouri River.

The Two Rivers

The Mississippi and the Missouri are important waterways. What would the United States be like without these two powerful rivers? How big an impact would it have on the lives of people? How big an impact would it have on the wildlife? Industry and commerce would suffer. Wildlife and ecosystems would disappear. Plants, animals, and fish that we think of as common might not exist.

Besides their scenic beauty, the rivers sustain a way of life for millions of people. From north to south, east to west, these two rivers are a part of American history and culture that has existed since before the days of the pioneers. They are both mighty rivers, although one may be a little muddy.

Life along the Mississippi River near Fountain City, Wisconsin

The beautiful city of St. Louis would not be the same without the two great rivers.

Now Try This

Study a River

In this book you read about two of the great rivers in the United States. Now it is time to find out about other great rivers.

1. Find a partner. Look at a map of the world. Pick out another major river in the United States or in another country in the world.

2. Next decide what you would like to learn about the river. Make a list of questions you have and choose questions to answer.

3. Now it is time to do research. Look at encyclopedias and other reference books for more information about the river you selected.

4. Assemble your findings in a format that you can present to the class. Include a map. Share your findings with the group and answer questions regarding your river.

Glossary

barges *n.* large, strongly built, flat-bottomed boats for carrying freight on rivers, canals, etc.

conservationists *n.* people who want to preserve and protect the forests, rivers, and other natural resources of a country.

diminishing *v.* making or becoming smaller.

expedition *n.* a journey for some special purpose, such as exploration, scientific study, or military purposes.

reservoirs *n.* places where water is collected and stored for use.

route *n.* a way to go; road.

silt *n.* very fine particles of dirt carried by moving water and deposited as sediment.

tributaries *n.* streams or rivers that flow into a lake or a larger river.